Copyright © 2022 Matthew Douglas Pinard

All Rights Reserved. No part of this book publication may be reproduced or transmitted in any form or by any means, mechanical or electronic, including photocopying, scanning, and recording, or by any information storage and retrieval system, or other -- without prior permission in writing from the author or publisher. Disclaimers: The Publisher and the Author make no representation or warranties concerning the accuracy or completeness of the contents of this work and specifically disclaim all warranties for a particular purpose. No warranty may be created or extended through sales or promotional materials. The advice and strategies contained herein may not be suitable for every situation. This work is sold with the understanding that the Author and Publisher are not engaged in rendering legal, technological, or other professional services. If professional assistance is required, the services of a competent professional should be sought. Neither the Publisher nor the Author shall be liable for damages arising therefrom. The fact that an organization or website is referred to in this work as a citation and/or potential source of further information does not mean that the Author or the Publisher endorses the information, the organization, or website it may provide, or recommendations it may make. Further, readers should be aware that the websites listed in this work may have changed or disappeared between the time that this work was written and when it is read. Details of the cases and stories in this book have been changed to preserve privacy.

Printed in the United States of America
Published by: Writer's Publishing House
Prescott, Az 86301

Cover and Interior Design by Creative Artistic Excellence Marketing
Project Management and Book Launch by Creative Artistic Excellence Marketing
https://lizzymcnett.com

Paperback ISBN: 978-1-64873-252-2
Hardcover ISBN: 978-1-64873-253-9
Ebook ISBN: 978-1-64873-254-6

The Blue Lady

Table of Contents

ROGER THE ANGEL — 5

EARTHLY BIRTHING PANGS — 14

MORE HORSES ON THE MARK — 17

SLYPHS SLIPPING THROUGH OUR SKIES — 21

THE MAY SYLPHS — 21

THE JUNE SLYPHS — 112

THE BLUE LADY — 248

THE AUGUST SLYPHS AND A FEW DEMONS — 397

MEET VIRGINIA — 442

CONCLUSION — 444

Other Books by Author Matthew Douglas Piard — 450

Screenplay Awards — 452

About Matthew Douglas Pinard — 454

ROGER THE ANGEL

On July 8th, 2021, the world lost an incredible man named Roger Dunigan.

Roger was a former Roman Catholic Priest who married my wife Carol Rose and I in July of 2008. He was a kind, funny, generous man who's loud and boisterous laugh I will never forget.

The man of incredible faith attended Catholic Mass frequently near a Native American reservation in northern Michigan up until his passing. He had a special love and interest in what he called "senior dogs", which he often rescued from animal shelters.

Jeanette, Roger's significant other is a kind and outgoing woman. Prior to his passing, I often joked with Roger, who knew he was dying from terminal prostate cancer, that before he went to heaven, he had to stop and say hello to my wife Carol and I in Arizona. The day after Roger's passing into life in the middle of the night of July 8th, 2021, brought a sunset I will never forget.

I believe Angel Roger said hello in a usually dramatic fashion.

Photo: A photo of our good friend Roger Dunigan prior to his passing on July 8th, 2021. There is no doubt Roger is now an Angel looking down on all of us.

Photo: An incredible image of an angel in flight on July 8th, 2021 above Prescott Valley, Arizona following the passing of a good friend named Roger Dunigan who married my wife and I in 2008.

Photo: An amazing image of an angel in flight looking back towards the left on July 8th, 2021 above Prescott Valley, Arizona following the passing of a good friend named Roger Dunigan.

Photo: An incredible image of what appears to be yet another horse head looking to the right above Prescott Valley, Arizona on July 8th, 2021. This appearance of yet another horse fits with the themes of my previous books that give evidence of the horsemen of the apocalypse.

Photo: An incredible image from the evening of July 8th, 2021 following the passing of a good friend named Roger Dunigan who married my wife and I in 2008. There is no doubt this is an angel in flight taking Roger to Heaven/Eden/ An. You can clearly see a smiling face to the top right on top of a wing lit by the setting sun.

Photo: An incredible sunset rich with red, orange and yellow hues appeared the evening of July 8th, 2021 following the passing of a good friend named Roger Dunigan who married my wife and I in 2008.

Photo: The morning of July 9th, 2021 above Prescott Valley, Arizona brought this incredible image of what to me appears as a face with white hair and beard. This image appeared while reciting a rosary for our friend Roger Dunigan who passed away on July 8th, 2021. I have no doubt this is Roger Dunigan looking down from heaven upon us. Roger was an incredible man of faith and former Catholic Priest who married my wife and I in 2008.

Photo: On the morning of July 9th, 2021 following the passing of a good friend named Roger Dunigan this beautiful yellow monarch butterfly appeared in our backyard and would not leave. The monarch butterfly is a sign of resurrection and change. I pray this is a sign for the entire world.

EARTHLY BIRTHING PANGS

Many describe the Apocalypse prophesied in the Book of Revelations as "birth pangs" bringing change to the earth.

The fact that our planet rests on a series of tectonic plates, and that volcanic activity has not only brought about changes in terrain, but also life to various species on the planet, further serves that these events, while often scary and seemingly unending, may be a new beginning.

Let's look at some recent undeniable events that appear on the surface to be apocalyptic in nature.

As of July 2021, there was massive flooding in Germany and China, resulting in hundreds of deaths. Yet headlines simultaneously stated mortality rates are the lowest since post World War II.

The world continues to see major earthquakes (at least one per day, magnitude 4.0 or greater). Massive heatwaves with temperatures never recorded have scorched the Pacific Northwest resulting in over 80 wildfires burning millions of acres that have threatened both lives and homes.

Photo: On June 1st, 2021 this incredible "all seeing eye" appeared in the skies above central Arizona. When I took this photo you could definitely feel like you were being watched from on high.

Photo: On June 10th, 2021 the world woke up to a "ring of fire" solar eclipse which produced beautiful images like the one above. I also found it very interesting as one news outlet wrote that the day after this event it was noted that at least twenty seven volcanoes along the Pacific "ring of fire" were erupting. Is this a coincidence?

MORE HORSES ON THE MARK

I found it interesting that three days after this apocalyptic ring of fire solar eclipse, we were given a glimpse of yet another apocalyptic series of horsemen.

I've taken numerous additional head horse photos since the ones seen in my previous books. The photo below shows what appears to me as a huge horse head at sunset, hinting at yet further evidence this planet is in a state of change.

Photo: The evening of June 13th, 2021 above Prescott Valley, Arizona shows an incredible setting sun with what appears as a large horse head to the left of the sun.

Photo: The evening of June 13th, 2021 above Prescott Valley, Arizona shows an incredible setting sun with what appears as a large horse head to the left of the sun. This is a blow up of the horse head. You can clearly see a nose to the right and eyes and mane towards the top of the frame. I have shown this to others who also see the same.

Photo: Another shot of from the evening of June 13th, 2021 above Prescott Valley, Arizona shows an incredible setting sun with what appears as a large horse head to the left of the sun. This is another blow up of the horse head. You can clearly see a nose to the right and eyes and mane towards the top of the frame. I have shown this to others who also see the same. There also appears to be an angel in flight behind the head to the top left of the frame.

SLYPHS SLIPPING THROUGH OUR SKIES

A great way to view in more depth is following my YouTube channel @Matthew Douglas Pinard.

I take both photos and videos of some of my best Angel filled skies.

In any event, I had a viewer comment on one of the videos stating, "Sylph's, air spirits, beautiful, thanks for sharing and noticing."

I found the comment wonderful, and had never heard the word "Sylph." By definition means "an imaginary spirit in the air."

The definition is fascinating, as I do not find my encounters with these spirits "imaginary", nor is it coincidental that their appearance is coming during very apocalyptic times for the world.

In any event, I wanted to include some of the best photos I've ever seen of "Sylph spirits" from May, June, July and August of 2021. Especially in the context from some of the apocalyptic events from these months of 2021.

For example, as of July 2021, there were more than 80 major wildfires covering over 3 million acres in the Pacific Northwest and parts of western Canada. There are still major volcanic eruptions simultaneously along the ring of fire simultaneously. I find this interesting, as our mainstream media continues to focus on the efforts of a few elite billionaires to escape into space flights.

One individual actually started on an online petition that has garnered hundreds of thousands of signatures, asking that billionaire and Amazon founder Jeff Bezos be not allowed to return to planet Earth after his launch into space in July 2021. While amusing, I believe this individual has captured the sentiments of many people struggling to simply pay the bills and hold down a steady job in the middle of a worldwide pandemic that has taken over 4 million lives. The spikes in a Delta variant of the virus, seemingly rendering the vaccinated vulnerable again.

My question is this, to what other planet or universe do the elites hope to escape to while we suffer this global apocalypse?

THE MAY SYLPHS

Photo: On May 22nd, 2021 this incredible spirit or "slyph" appeared directly above Sacred Heart Catholic Church in Prescott, Arizona while I was on my way into the church to say a rosary for world peace and for the world to turn away from war and greed.

Photo: On May 22nd, 2021 another incredible spirit or "slyph" appeared directly above Sacred Heart Catholic Church in Prescott, Arizona while I was on my way into the church to say a rosary for world peace and for the world to turn away from war and greed. I can see two eyes within a face in the middle of the frame.

Photo: On May 22nd, 2021 this incredible huge winged "slyph" appeared directly above our home in Prescott Valley, Arizona following a rosary for world peace and for the world to turn away from war and greed.

Photo: On May 22nd, 2021 another incredible huge winged "slyph" appeared directly above our home in Prescott Valley, Arizona following a rosary for world peace and for the world to turn away from war and greed.

Photo: On May 25th, 2021 another incredible huge winged "slyph" appeared directly above our home in Prescott Valley, Arizona following a rosary for world peace and for the world to turn away from war and greed.

Photo: On May 25th, 2021 another incredible huge winged "slyph" appeared directly above our home in Prescott Valley, Arizona following a rosary for world peace and for the world to turn away from war and greed.

Photo: On May 25th, 2021 another incredible huge winged "slyph" appeared directly above our home in Prescott Valley, Arizona following a rosary for world peace and for the world to turn away from war and greed.

Photo: On May 25th, 2021 another incredible huge winged "slyph" appeared directly above our neighborhood in Prescott Valley, Arizona following a rosary for world peace and for the world to turn away from war and greed.

Photo: On May 25th, 2021 another incredible huge winged "slyph" appeared directly above our home in Prescott Valley, Arizona following a rosary for world peace and for the world to turn away from war and greed.

Photo: On May 25th, 2021 another incredible huge winged "slyph" appeared directly above our home in Prescott Valley, Arizona following a rosary for world peace and for the world to turn away from war and greed. This particular angelic spirit is multi-colored and clearly possessing two wings.

Photo: On May 25th, 2021 another incredible huge winged "slyph" appeared directly above our home in Prescott Valley, Arizona following a rosary for world peace and for the world to turn away from war and greed.

Photo: On May 25th, 2021 another incredible huge winged "slyph" appeared directly above Sacred Heart Catholic Church in Prescott, Arizona following a rosary for world peace and for the world to turn away from war and greed.

Photo: On May 25th, 2021 another incredible huge winged "slyph" appeared directly above our home in Prescott Valley, Arizona following a rosary for world peace and for the world to turn away from war and greed. This angelic spirit has a face near the top middle of the frame that appears to be looking down towards the right of the frame.

Photo: On May 25th, 2021 another incredible huge winged "slyph" appeared directly above our home in Prescott Valley, Arizona following a rosary for world peace and for the world to turn away from war and greed. This angelic spirit has a face near the top middle of the frame that appears to be looking to the left of the frame mouth wide open.

Photo: On May 25th, 2021 another incredible huge winged "slyph" appeared directly above our home in Prescott Valley, Arizona following a rosary for world peace and for the world to turn away from war and greed. This angelic spirit clearly has a body with wings and is also multi-colored.

Photo: On May 25th, 2021 another incredible huge winged "slyph" appeared directly above our home in Prescott Valley, Arizona following a rosary for world peace and for the world to turn away from war and greed. This angelic spirit has a face near the middle of the frame that appears to be looking straight at the camera.

Photo: On May 26th, 2021 another incredible huge winged "slyph" appeared directly above our home in Prescott Valley, Arizona following a rosary for world peace and for the world to turn away from war and greed. This angelic spirit has a face near the top middle of the frame that appears to be looking down towards the left of the frame with wings open in flight.

Photo: On May 26th, 2021 another incredible huge winged "slyph" appeared directly above our home in Prescott Valley, Arizona following a rosary for world peace and for the world to turn away from war and greed.

Photo: On May 26th, 2021 another incredible huge winged "slyph" appeared directly above our home in Prescott Valley, Arizona following a rosary for world peace and for the world to turn away from war and greed.

Photo: On May 26th, 2021 another incredible huge winged "slyph" appeared directly above our home in Prescott Valley, Arizona following a rosary for world peace and for the world to turn away from war and greed. This angelic spirit has a face near the top middle of the frame that appears to be looking straight at the camera.

Photo: On May 26th, 2021 another incredible huge winged "slyph" appeared directly above Prescott Valley, Arizona following a rosary for world peace and for the world to turn away from war and greed. This angelic spirit has a face near the top middle of the frame that appears to be looking down the right.

Photo: On May 26th, 2021 another incredible huge winged "slyph" appeared directly above our home in Prescott Valley, Arizona following a rosary for world peace and for the world to turn away from war and greed. This angelic spirit has a face near the right of the frame that appears to be looking straight at the camera.

Photo: On May 26th, 2021 another incredible huge winged "slyph" appeared directly above Prescott Valley, Arizona following a rosary for world peace and for the world to turn away from war and greed. I see multiple faces in this slyph spirit, one to the far right looks like a bull steer to me or cow's head.

Photo: On May 26th, 2021 another incredible huge winged "slyph" appeared directly above our home in Prescott Valley, Arizona following a rosary for world peace and for the world to turn away from war and greed. This angelic spirit has a face near the top middle of the frame that appears to be looking straight at the camera and also appears to me as yet another horse head of the apocalypse.

Photo: On May 26th, 2021 another incredible huge winged "slyph" appeared directly above our home in Prescott Valley, Arizona following a rosary for world peace and for the world to turn away from war and greed. This angelic spirit has a face near the middle of the frame that appears to be looking straight at the camera.

Photo: On May 26th, 2021 another incredible huge winged "slyph" appeared directly above our home in Prescott Valley, Arizona following a rosary for world peace and for the world to turn away from war and greed.

Photo: On May 26th, 2021 another incredible huge winged "slyph" appeared directly above our home in Prescott Valley, Arizona following a rosary for world peace and for the world to turn away from war and greed. This angelic spirit has a face near the top middle of the frame that appears to be looking up to the right of the frame. There are other faces near the bottom as well.

Photo: On May 26th, 2021 another incredible huge winged "slyph" appeared directly above our home in Prescott Valley, Arizona following a rosary for world peace and for the world to turn away from war and greed. This angelic spirit has a face near the top middle of the frame that appears to be looking up to the right of the frame. There are also other faces near the bottom as well.

Photo: On May 26th, 2021 another incredible huge blue winged "slyph" appeared directly above Prescott Valley, Arizona following a rosary for world peace and for the world to turn away from war and greed.

Photo: On May 26th, 2021 another incredible huge blue winged "slyph" appeared directly above Prescott Valley, Arizona following a rosary for world peace and for the world to turn away from war and greed.

Photo: On May 28th, 2021 another incredible huge blue winged "slyph" appeared directly above Prescott Valley, Arizona following a rosary for world peace and for the world to turn away from war and greed. This was also interesting considering we had another super pink moon on May 28th, 2021.

Photo: On May 29th, 2021 another incredible huge blue winged "slyph" appeared directly above Prescott Valley, Arizona following a rosary for world peace and for the world to turn away from war and greed.

Photo: On May 29th, 2021 another incredible huge blue winged "slyph" appeared directly above Prescott Valley, Arizona following a rosary for world peace and for the world to turn away from war and greed. If you look to the top left you can see a figure with wings outstretched.

Photo: On May 29th, 2021 another incredible huge blue faced "slyph" appeared directly above Prescott Valley, Arizona following a rosary for world peace and for the world to turn away from war and greed. If you look closely you can see a face with two eyes and mouth to the bottom right.

Photo: On May 29th, 2021 another incredible huge blue horse head "slyph" appeared directly above Prescott Valley, Arizona following a rosary for world peace and for the world to turn away from war and greed. If you look closely you can see a horse head with two eyes and mouth to the bottom right. Is this yet another horse of the apocalypse?

Photo: On May 29th, 2021 another incredible "slyph" appeared directly above Prescott Valley, Arizona following a rosary for world peace and for the world to turn away from war and greed. If you look closely you can see a face with two eyes and mouth to the bottom right with a blue figure to its left.

Photo: On May 29th, 2021 another incredible "slyph" face arms outstretched appeared directly above Prescott Valley, Arizona following a rosary for world peace and for the world to turn away from war and greed. If you look closely you can see a face with two eyes and mouth to the top left of the frame.

Photo: On May 29th, 2021 another incredible "slyph" face with eyes and mouth appeared directly above Prescott Valley, Arizona following a rosary for world peace and for the world to turn away from war and greed. If you look closely you can see a face with two eyes and mouth to the top middle of the frame.

Photo: On May 29th, 2021 another incredible huge winged "slyph" covered the entire skies directly above Prescott Valley, Arizona following a rosary for world peace and for the world to turn away from war and greed.

Photo: On May 29th, 2021 another incredible "slyph" face appeared directly above Prescott Valley, Arizona following a rosary for world peace and for the world to turn away from war and greed. If you look closely you can see a face with two eyes and mouth to the middle of the frame.

Photo: On May 29th, 2021 another incredible "slyph" blue face appeared directly above Prescott Valley, Arizona following a rosary for world peace and for the world to turn away from war and greed. If you look closely you can see a face with two eyes and mouth to the middle of the frame that almost looks like a dog to me.

Photo: On May 29th, 2021 another incredible "slyph" group of faces appeared directly above Prescott Valley, Arizona following a rosary for world peace and for the world to turn away from war and greed.

Photo: On May 29th, 2021 another incredible "slyph" white rabbit face appeared directly above my neighbors home in Prescott Valley, Arizona following a rosary for world peace and for the world to turn away from war and greed.

Photo: On May 29th, 2021 another incredible "slyph" white face within a face appeared directly above my neighborhood in Prescott Valley, Arizona following a rosary for world peace and for the world to turn away from war and greed.

Photo: On May 29th, 2021 another incredible "slyph" face within a face appeared directly above my house in Prescott Valley, Arizona following a rosary for world peace and for the world to turn away from war and greed.

Photo: On May 29th, 2021 another set of incredible "slyph" faces appeared directly above my house in Prescott Valley, Arizona following a rosary for world peace and for the world to turn away from war and greed.

Photo: On May 29th, 2021 another set of incredible "slyph" faces and wings appeared directly above my house in Prescott Valley, Arizona following a rosary for world peace and for the world to turn away from war and greed.

Photo: On May 29th, 2021 another set of incredible "slyph" faces and wings appeared directly above my house in Prescott Valley, Arizona following a rosary for world peace and for the world to turn away from war and greed.

Photo: On May 29th, 2021 another set of incredible "slyph" faces and wings appeared directly above my house in Prescott Valley, Arizona following a rosary for world peace and for the world to turn away from war and greed.

Photo: On May 29th, 2021 another set of incredible "slyph" faces and wings appeared directly above my house in Prescott Valley, Arizona following a rosary for world peace and for the world to turn away from war and greed.

Photo: On May 29th, 2021 another set of incredible "slyph" faces and wings appeared directly above my house in Prescott Valley, Arizona following a rosary for world peace and for the world to turn away from war and greed.

Photo: On May 29th, 2021 another set of incredible "slyph" faces and wings appeared directly above my house in Prescott Valley, Arizona following a rosary for world peace and for the world to turn away from war and greed.

Photo: On May 29th, 2021 another set of incredible "slyph" faces and wings appeared directly above my house in Prescott Valley, Arizona following a rosary for world peace and for the world to turn away from war and greed.

Photo: On May 29th, 2021 another set of incredible "slyph" faces and wings appeared directly above my house in Prescott Valley, Arizona following a rosary for world peace and for the world to turn away from war and greed.

Photo: On May 29th, 2021 another set of incredible "slyph" faces and wings appeared directly above my house in Prescott Valley, Arizona following a rosary for world peace and for the world to turn away from war and greed.

Photo: On May 29th, 2021 another set of incredible "slyph" faces and wings appeared directly above my house in Prescott Valley, Arizona following a rosary for world peace and for the world to turn away from war and greed.

Photo: On May 29th, 2021 another huge winged "slyph" appeared directly above my house in Prescott Valley, Arizona following a rosary for world peace and for the world to turn away from war and greed.

Photo: On May 29th, 2021 another set of incredible "slyph" faces and wings appeared directly above my house in Prescott Valley, Arizona following a rosary for world peace and for the world to turn away from war and greed. You can see a huge angel wing to the bottom middle of the frame and a face to the top left of the wing.

Photo: On May 29th, 2021 another set of incredible "slyph" wings appeared directly above my house in Prescott Valley, Arizona following a rosary for world peace and for the world to turn away from war and greed.

Photo: On May 31st, 2021 another set of incredible "slyph" faces and wings appeared directly above my house in Prescott Valley, Arizona following a rosary for world peace and for the world to turn away from war and greed. You can see a huge angel wing to the middle of the frame and a face to the top left and right of the wing.

Photo: On May 31st, 2021 another set of incredible "slyph" faces and wings appeared directly above my house in Prescott Valley, Arizona following a rosary for world peace and for the world to turn away from war and greed.

Photo: On May 31st, 2021 another set of incredible image of what appeared to me to be two humpback whales floating through the skies directly above my house in Prescott Valley, Arizona following a rosary for world peace and for the world to turn away from war and greed.

Photo: On May 31st, 2021 I attended a mass at Sacred Heart Catholic Church in Prescott, Arizona and took a picture of the cover art on the bulletin. Take a close look at this artwork. There is a triangle above God the Father who is seated next to The Son Jesus Christ and a White Wing Dove above them. This is further evidence we are descendants of an alien race responsible for our DNA and for the design of the ancient pyramids.

Photo: On May 31st, 2021 another set of incredible "slyph" faces and wings appeared directly above my house in Prescott Valley, Arizona following a rosary for world peace and for the world to turn away from war and greed. You can see a huge angel wing to the middle of the frame and a face to the top left and right of the wing.

Photo: On May 31st, 2021 another set of incredible "slyph" faces and wings appeared directly above my house in Prescott Valley, Arizona following a rosary for world peace and for the world to turn away from war and greed.

Photo: On May 31st, 2021 another set of incredible "slyph" face appeared directly above my house in Prescott Valley, Arizona following a rosary for world peace and for the world to turn away from war and greed.

Photo: On May 31st, 2021 another set of incredible "slyph" faces and wings appeared directly above my house in Prescott Valley, Arizona following a rosary for world peace and for the world to turn away from war and greed.

Photo: On May 31st, 2021 another set of incredible "slyph" angel appeared directly above my house in Prescott Valley, Arizona following a rosary for world peace and for the world to turn away from war and greed. You can see a huge angel that seems to be flexing his left bicep and looking back to the left.

Photo: On May 31st, 2021 another incredible "slyph" angel appeared directly above my neighborhood in Prescott Valley, Arizona following a rosary for world peace and for the world to turn away from war and greed. You can see a huge angel that seems to be on its back looking back to its right and its right wing facing the sky. I call these "Rain Angels" or "Raingels" because they usually bring much needed rain to our dry state of Arizona.

Photo: On May 31st, 2021 another set of incredible "slyph" angel appeared directly above my house in Prescott Valley, Arizona following a rosary for world peace and for the world to turn away from war and greed. You can see a huge angel that seems to be holding a baby below it and one that has simultaneously taken the shape of a lobster's claw.

Photo: On May 31st, 2021 another set of incredible "slyph" angels one following the other appeared directly above my house in Prescott Valley, Arizona following a rosary for world peace and for the world to turn away from war and greed.

Photo: On May 31st, 2021 another set of incredible "slyph" angels appeared directly above my house in Prescott Valley, Arizona following a rosary for world peace and for the world to turn away from war and greed. You can see a huge cross with multiple faces on it floating above us. One face in the middle seems to be rather angry, but yet "exorcised."

Photo: On May 31st, 2021 another incredible "slyph" angel appeared directly above my house in Prescott Valley, Arizona following a rosary for world peace and for the world to turn away from war and greed. You can see a huge face looking to the left while wearing some kind of hat. The Angel's ear, face, lips and eyes and nose.

Photo: On May 31st, 2021 another incredible "slyph" angel appeared directly above my house in Prescott Valley, Arizona following a rosary for world peace and for the world to turn away from war and greed. You can see a huge angel that seems to be hovering with two wings, a face that appears to be looking at the camera.

Photo: On May 31st, 2021 another set of incredible "slyph" angels appeared directly above my house in Prescott Valley, Arizona following a rosary for world peace and for the world to turn away from war and greed. You can see two huge angels one hovering above the other looking to the right.

Photo: On May 31st, 2021 another set of incredible "slyph" angels appeared directly above my house in Prescott Valley, Arizona following a rosary for world peace and for the world to turn away from war and greed. You can see a huge angel that seems to be looking back over its right shoulder at two hovering faces.

Photo: On May 31st, 2021 another incredible "slyph" angel appeared directly above my house in Prescott Valley, Arizona following a rosary for world peace and for the world to turn away from war and greed. You can see a huge angel face top middle with what appears oddly to be a pair of bunny ears on its head.

Photo: On May 31st, 2021 another set of incredible "slyph" angels appeared directly above Prescott Valley, Arizona following a rosary for world peace and for the world to turn away from war and greed. You can see a group of rain angels or "raingles" that seems to be hovering above a large wing bringing rain.

Photo: On May 31st, 2021 another set of incredible "slyph" angels appeared directly above Prescott Valley, Arizona following a rosary for world peace and for the world to turn away from war and greed. You can see an angel hovering above another one.

Photo: On May 31st, 2021 another set of incredible "slyph" angels appeared directly above Prescott Valley, Arizona following a rosary for world peace and for the world to turn away from war and greed. You can see multiple faces and wings outstretched.

Photo: On May 31st, 2021 another set of incredible "slyph" angels appeared directly above Prescott Valley, Arizona following a rosary for world peace and for the world to turn away from war and greed. You can clearly see a head on the leading right edge brining rain beneath it.

Photo: On May 31st, 2021 another set of incredible "slyph" angels appeared directly above Prescott Valley, Arizona following a rosary for world peace and for the world to turn away from war and greed. You can see a face with eyes in the middle of the frame.

Photo: On May 31st, 2021 another set of incredible "slyph" angels appeared directly above Prescott Valley, Arizona following a rosary for world peace and for the world to turn away from war and greed. The angels seem to be facing in towards a blue baby angel.

Photo: On May 31st, 2021 another set of incredible "slyph" angels appeared directly above Prescott Valley, Arizona following a rosary for world peace and for the world to turn away from war and greed. The middle angel has a large head with eyes looking to its right shoulder/ wing.

Photo: On May 31st, 2021 another set of incredible "slyph" angels appeared directly above Prescott Valley, Arizona following a rosary for world peace and for the world to turn away from war and greed. There is a face in the top middle of the frame with two eyes.

Photo: On May 31st, 2021 another set of incredible "slyph" angels appeared directly above Prescott Valley, Arizona following a rosary for world peace and for the world to turn away from war and greed. There is a large face and a smaller face in the middle of the frame.

Photo: On May 31st, 2021 another set of incredible "slyph" angels appeared directly above Prescott Valley, Arizona following a rosary for world peace and for the world to turn away from war and greed. There is a large angel face to the right of the frame dumping rain above our dry valley. Yet another example of rain angel or "Raingel."

Photo: On May 31st, 2021 another set of incredible "slyph" angels appeared directly above Prescott Valley, Arizona following a rosary for world peace and for the world to turn away from war and greed. This is another rain angel or "Raingel" as you can see a huge face in the top center smiling to its left as it delivers rain to our dry valley.

Photo: On May 31st, 2021 another set of incredible "slyph" angels appeared directly above Prescott Valley, Arizona following a rosary for world peace and for the world to turn away from war and greed at sunset. In this image I believe there is a fallen angel or demon within another fallen angel/demon face. You can clearly see eyes, ears, and a goatee hanging down. This was yet another sign the light is winning vs. the dark.

THE JUNE SLYPHS

June of 2021 brought an enormous amount of Angel Slyph paranormal activity to central Arizona as well as other states like Colorado and Utah I visited for my job.

Photo: This amazing slyph of an angelic face staring upwards was taken near Logan, Utah on June 1st, 2021 on my way to work with local retina surgeons.

Photo: This amazing slyph of an angelic face and wing was taken near Salt Lake City, Utah on June 1st, 2021 on my way to work with local retina surgeons.

Photo: This amazing slyph of an angelic face and wing was taken near Salt Lake City, Utah at sunset June 1st, 2021 on my way to work with local retina surgeons.

Photo: This amazing slyph of an angelic face and wing was taken near Salt Lake City, Utah on June 2nd, 2021 on my way to work with local retina surgeons.

Photo: This amazing slyph of an angelic wing was taken near Salt Lake City, Utah on June 2nd, 2021 on my way to work with local retina surgeons.

Photo: This amazing slyph of an angelic wing was taken near Prescott Valley, Arizona on June 6th, 2021 after a morning rosary for world peace and for the world to turn away from war and greed.

Photo: This amazing slyph of an angelic wing and face was taken near Prescott Valley, Arizona on June 7th, 2021 after a morning rosary for world peace and for the world to turn away from war and greed.

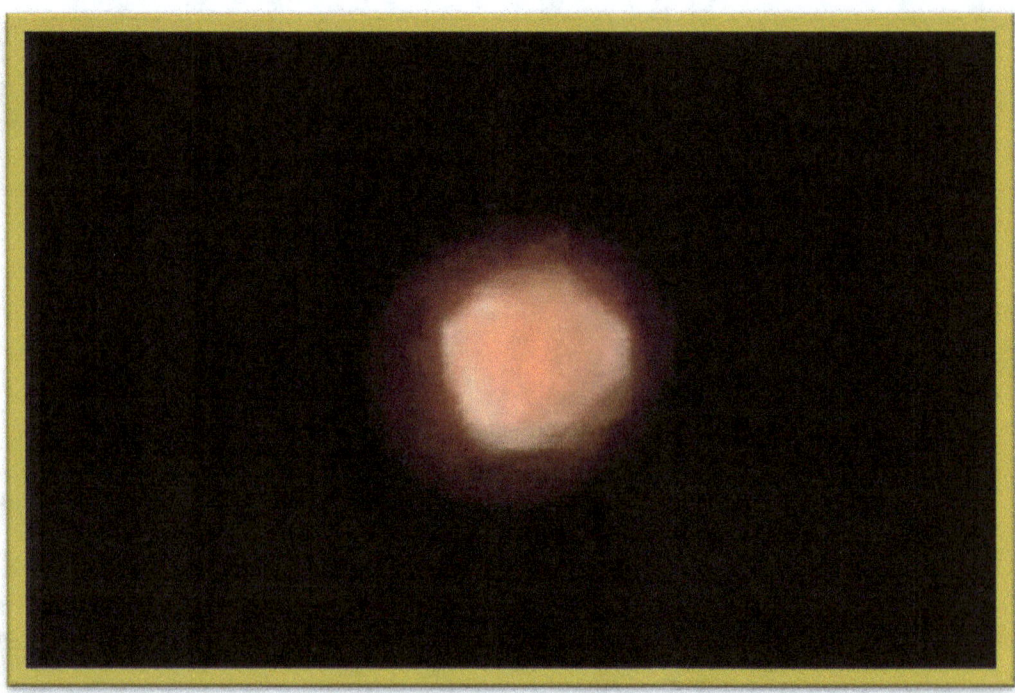

Photo: This mysterious light was taken near Prescott Valley, Arizona on June 9th, 2021 after a morning rosary for world peace and for the world to turn away from war and greed.

Photo: This amazing slyph of an angelic wing was taken near Salt Lake City, Utah on June 9th, 2021 after a morning rosary for world peace and for the world to turn away from war and greed. You can see a face near the middle of the frame with wings outstretched.

Photo: This amazing slyph of an angelic wing and face was taken near Salt Lake City, Utah on June 9th, 2021 after a morning rosary for world peace and for the world to turn away from war and greed.

Photo: This amazing slyph of an angelic wing was taken near Salt Lake City, Utah on June 9th, 2021 after a morning rosary for world peace and for the world to turn away from war and greed.

Photo: This amazing slyph of an angelic face wings outstretched was taken near Prescott Valley, Arizona at sunset on June 12th, 2021 after a morning rosary for world peace and for the world to turn away from war and greed. You can see a face near the middle of the frame with wings outstretched.

Photo: This amazing slyph of an angelic wing was taken near Prescott Valley, Arizona on June 13th, 2021 after a morning rosary for world peace and for the world to turn away from war and greed.

Photo: This amazing slyph of an angelic face and wing was taken near Prescott Valley, Arizona on June 13th, 2021 after a morning rosary for world peace and for the world to turn away from war and greed.

Photo: This amazing slyph of an angelic wing was taken near Prescott Valley, Arizona on June 13th, 2021 after a morning rosary for world peace and for the world to turn away from war and greed.

Photo: This amazing slyph of an angelic face and wing was taken near Prescott Valley, Arizona on June 13th, 2021 after a morning rosary for world peace and for the world to turn away from war and greed.

Photo: This amazing slyph of an angelic wing with multiple faces was taken above my roof in Prescott Valley, Arizona on June 15th, 2021 after a morning rosary for world peace and for the world to turn away from war and greed. You can see a face near the middle of the frame with wings outstretched.

Photo: This amazing slyph of an angelic wing with multiple faces was taken above my roof in Prescott Valley, Arizona on June 15th, 2021 after a morning rosary for world peace and for the world to turn away from war and greed. You can see a face near the middle of the frame with wings outstretched.

Photo: This amazing slyph of an angelic body with wings flapping in the air was taken above my roof in Prescott Valley, Arizona on June 15th, 2021 after a morning rosary for world peace and for the world to turn away from war and greed. You can see a face and body near the middle of the frame with wings outstretched.

Photo: This amazing slyph of an angelic body with wings flapping in the air (top right) and zoomed out to reveal a larger wing and slyph angel was taken above my roof in Prescott Valley, Arizona on June 15th, 2021 after a morning rosary for world peace and for the world to turn away from war and greed.

Photo: This amazing slyph of an angelic body, face and wings was taken in Prescott Valley, Arizona on June 15th, 2021 after a morning rosary for world peace and for the world to turn away from war and greed. You can see a face and body near the middle of the frame with wings outstretched.

Photo: This amazing slyph sunset was taken above my roof in Prescott Valley, Arizona on June 15th, 2021 after a morning rosary for world peace and for the world to turn away from war and greed. You can see two large angel slyph faces top right of the frame.

Photo: This amazing sunset was taken above Prescott Valley, Arizona on June 15th, 2021 after a morning rosary for world peace and for the world to turn away from war and greed. This amazing view reminded me of something out of a Star Wars movie of another world.

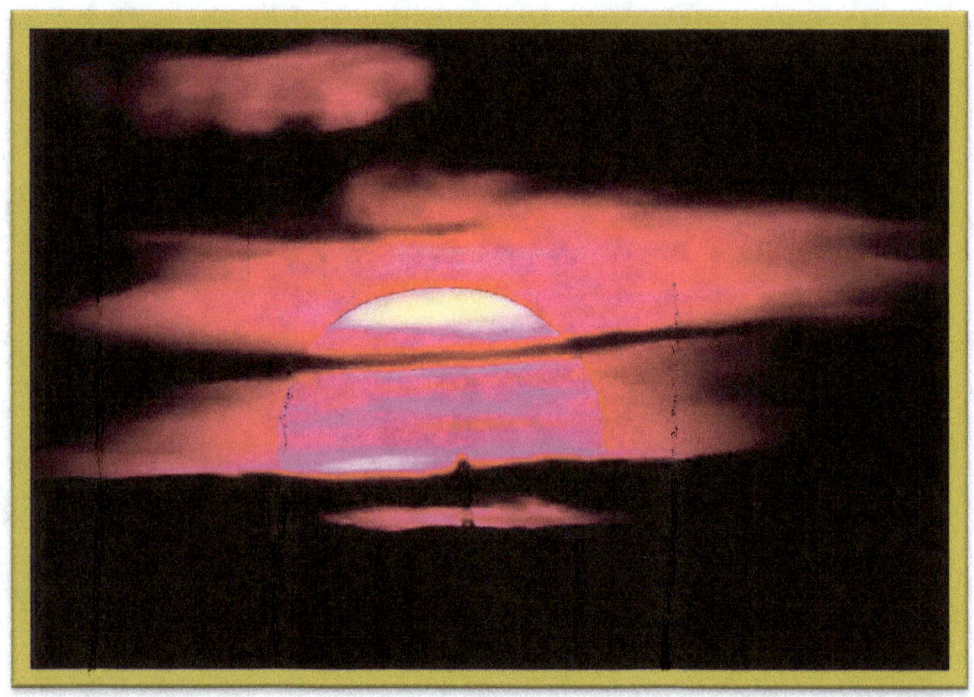

Photo: This amazing sunset was taken above Prescott Valley, Arizona on June 15th, 2021 after a morning rosary for world peace and for the world to turn away from war and greed. This amazing view of a red sun setting reminded me of something out of a Star Wars movie of another world.

Photo: This amazing slyph angel with a huge face and wings outstretched was taken above my roof in Prescott Valley, Arizona on June 18th, 2021 after a morning rosary for world peace and for the world to turn away from war and greed.

Photo: This amazing sunset was taken above Prescott Valley, Arizona on June 18th, 2021 (the date of my sister Kate's birthday) after a morning rosary for world peace and for the world to turn away from war and greed. This looks like a huge slyph angel wing covered by clouds, backlit by the sun.

Photo: This amazing sunset was taken above Prescott Valley, Arizona on June 18th, 2021 (the date of my sister Kate's birthday) after a morning rosary for world peace and for the world to turn away from war and greed. This amazing sylph angel is holding its arms out to heaven and wings outstretched towards the sun.

Photo: This amazing sunset was taken above Prescott Valley, Arizona on June 18th, 2021 (the date of my sister Kate's birthday) after a morning rosary for world peace and for the world to turn away from war and greed.

Photo: A view of an amazing angel slyph in flight taken above Boulder, Colorado on June 24th, 2021 while on a business trip for my job as a surgical retina sales representative. This was another beautiful sign that the angel slyphs do follow us as protection. There is a hovering angel slyph face in this frame.

Photo: A view of an amazing angel slyph in flight taken above Boulder, Colorado on June 24th, 2021 while on a business trip for my job as a surgical retina sales representative. This was another beautiful sign that the angel slyphs do follow us as protection. This appears to me as two angel slyphs facing off against each other almost in a competition.

Photo: A view of an amazing angel slyph in flight taken above Boulder, Colorado on June 24th, 2021 while on a business trip for my job as a surgical retina sales representative. This was another beautiful sign that the angel slyphs do follow us as protection. This appears to me as a large blue angel slyph face above an all-seeing eye.

Photo: A view of an amazing angel slyph in flight taken above Boulder, Colorado on June 24th, 2021 while on a business trip for my job as a surgical retina sales representative. This was another beautiful sign that the angel slyphs do follow us as protection. This appears to me as a large angel head top middle of the frame above an outstretched wing.

Photo: A view of an amazing angel slyph in flight taken above Boulder, Colorado on June 24th, 2021 while on a business trip for my job as a surgical retina sales representative. This was another beautiful sign that the angel slyphs do follow us as protection. This appears to me as a large dark blue angel slyph wing at sunset.

Photo: A view of an amazing angel slyph in flight taken above Boulder, Colorado on June 24th, 2021 while on a business trip for my job as a surgical retina sales representative. This was another beautiful sign that the angel slyphs do follow us as protection. This appears to me as a very large angel slyph face.

Photo: A view of an amazing angel slyph in flight taken above Boulder, Colorado on June 24th, 2021 while on a business trip for my job as a surgical retina sales representative. This was another beautiful sign that the angel slyphs do follow us as protection. There is a hovering angel face with two wings outstretched in this frame.

Photo: A view of an amazing angel slyph in flight taken above Boulder, Colorado on June 24th, 2021 while on a business trip for my job as a surgical retina sales representative. This was another beautiful sign that the angel slyphs do follow us as protection. There is a hovering angel with two wings outstretched in this frame.

Photo: A view of an amazing angel slyph in flight taken above Boulder, Colorado on June 25th, 2021 while on a business trip for my job as a surgical retina sales representative. This was another beautiful sign that the angel slyphs do follow us as protection. This giant wing appeared as I walked out of my hotel room. It was as if it was there watching over me.

Photo: A view of an amazing angel slyph in flight taken above Boulder, Colorado on June 25th, 2021 while on a business trip for my job as a surgical retina sales representative. This was another beautiful sign that the angel slyphs do follow us as protection. This appears to me as a very large angel slyph face dead center of the frame.

Photo: A view of an amazing angel slyph sunset taken above Denver, Colorado on June 25th, 2021 while on a business trip for my job as a surgical retina sales representative. This was another beautiful sign that the angel slyphs do follow us as protection.

Photo: A view of an amazing angel slyph in flight taken above Denver, Colorado on the morning of June 25th, 2021 while on a business trip for my job as a surgical retina sales representative. This was another beautiful sign that the angel slyphs do follow us as protection. This appears to me to be a very large angel slyph face dead center of the frame. This face greeted me as I walked out of my hotel.

Photo: A view of an amazing angel slyph in flight taken above Boulder, Colorado on June 25th, 2021 while on a business trip for my job as a surgical retina sales representative. This was another beautiful sign that the angel slyphs do follow us as protection. This appears to me as a very large angel slyph dog face.

Photo: A view of an amazing angel slyph in flight taken above Prescott Valley, Arizona on June 26th, 2021, the date of my brother's birthday. This was another beautiful sign that the angel slyphs do follow us as protection. This appears to me as another very large blue angel slyph face in flight.

Photo: A view of an amazing angel slyph sunset taken above Prescott Valley, Arizona on June 26th, 2021, the date of my brother's birthday.

Photo: A view of an amazing angel slyph in flight taken above Prescott Valley, Arizona on June 26th, 2021, the date of my brother's birthday. This was another beautiful sign that the angel slyphs do follow us as protection. This appears to me as a very large blue angel slyph with wings in flight.

Photo: A view of an amazing angel slyph sunset taken above Prescott Valley, Arizona on June 26th, 2021, the date of my brother's birthday.

Photo: A view of an amazing angel slyph wings spread in flight taken above Prescott Valley, Arizona on June 28th, 2021 while on vacation with family.

Photo: A view of an amazing angel slyph wings spread in flight taken above Prescott Valley, Arizona on June 28th, 2021 while on vacation with family. You can clearly see a large face to the left looking left and a wing to the top and bottom right of the frame.

Photo: A view of an amazing angel slyph sunset taken above Prescott Valley, Arizona on June 28th, 2021 while on vacation with family.

Photo: A view of an amazing angel slyph wing spread in flight taken above Prescott Valley, Arizona on June 29th, 2021 while on vacation with family.

Photo: A view of an amazing blue angel slyph wing spread in flight taken above Prescott Valley, Arizona on June 29th, 2021 while on vacation with family. Notice the green orb top left.

Photo: A view of an amazing angel slyph large face with headdress taken above Prescott Valley, Arizona on June 29th, 2021 while on vacation with family.

Photo: A view of an amazing angel slyph smiling face taken above Lake Havasu, Arizona on June 29th, 2021 while on vacation with family.

Photo: A view of an amazing angel slyph smiling face taken above Lake Havasu, Arizona on June 30th, 2021 while on vacation with family.

Photo: A view of an amazing angel slyph giant wing taken above Lake Havasu, Arizona on June 30th, 2021 while on vacation with family.

Photo: A view of an amazing angel slyphs in flight above Lake Havasu, Arizona on June 30th, 2021 while on vacation with family.

Photo: This incredible angel slyph wing appeared above Lake Havasu, Arizona on July 1st, 2021 during a boating trip with family members for vacation. The wing is absolutely beautiful and enormous.

Photo: This incredible angel slyph face appeared above Lake Havasu, Arizona on July 1st, 2021 during a boating trip with family members for vacation.

Photo: This incredible angel slyph face looking to the right appeared above Lake Havasu, Arizona on July 1st, 2021 during a boating trip with family members for vacation.

Photo: This incredible angel slyph face flying with wings and looking to the right appeared above Sedona, Arizona on July 1st, 2021 during a trip with family members for vacation.

Photo: This incredible and mysterious angel slyph sunset appeared above Sedona, Arizona on July 2nd, 2021 during a trip with family members for vacation.

Photo: This incredible huge angel slyph wing appeared above Prescott Valley, Arizona on July 4th, 2021 during a trip with family members for vacation.

Photo: This incredible huge angel slyph wing appeared above Prescott Valley, Arizona on July 4th, 2021 during a trip with family members for vacation.

Photo: This incredible huge angel slyph appeared above Prescott Valley, Arizona on July 4th, 2021 during a trip with family members for vacation. If you look at the top left of the cloud you can see a large face looking to the left.

Photo: This incredible huge angel slyph wing appeared above Prescott Valley, Arizona on July 4th, 2021 during a trip with family members for vacation.

Photo: This incredible huge pair of angel slyph wings appeared above Prescott Valley, Arizona on July 4th, 2021 during a trip with family members for vacation.

Photo: This incredible pair of huge angel slyph wings appeared above Prescott Valley, Arizona on July 4th, 2021 during a trip with family members for vacation. It appears to me as is one is chasing the other.

Photo: This incredible huge angel slyph face and wing appeared above Prescott Valley, Arizona on July 4th, 2021 during a trip with family members for vacation. You can see a face clearly top left.

Photo: This incredible huge angel slyph wing appeared above Prescott Valley, Arizona on July 4th, 2021 during a hike with my wife Carol Rose. You can see the slyph face to the far left.

Photo: This incredible huge angel slyph wing appeared above Prescott Valley, Arizona on July 4th, 2021 during a hike with my wife Carol Rose.

Photo: This incredible huge angel slyph wing and face appeared above Prescott Valley, Arizona on July 4th, 2021 during a hike with my wife Carol Rose. This one appears to be scowling in the middle of the frame.

Photo: This incredible huge angel slyph wing and face appeared above Prescott Valley, Arizona on July 4th, 2021 during a hike with my wife Carol Rose. This one appears to be flying to the right in flight.

Photo: This incredible huge angel slyph pair of wings appeared above Prescott Valley, Arizona on July 4th, 2021 during a hike with my wife Carol Rose. This one appears to be flying to the right.

Photo: This incredible huge angel slyph appeared above Prescott Valley, Arizona on July 4th, 2021 during a hike with my wife Carol Rose. This one appears to be flying to the left looking backwards.

Photo: This beautiful angel slyph sunset appeared above Prescott Valley, Arizona on July 4th, 2021 after a hike with my wife Carol Rose. There is a very bright purple and yellow orb above the sun.

Photo: This beautiful angel slyph face appeared above Prescott Valley, Arizona on July 4th, 2021 after a hike with my wife Carol Rose.

Photo: This is a close up of the beautiful angel slyph face appeared above Prescott Valley, Arizona on July 4th, 2021 after a hike with my wife Carol Rose.

Photo: This beautiful and quite mysterious looking angel slyph sunset appeared above Prescott Valley, Arizona on July 4th, 2021 after a hike with my wife Carol Rose.

Photo: This beautiful angel slyph face appeared above Prescott Valley, Arizona on July 5th, 2021.

Photo: This beautiful pair of angel slyph faces smiling at each other appeared above Prescott Valley, Arizona on July 5th, 2021.

Photo: This is an incredible image of an exploding mud volcano in the Caspian Sea on July 5th, 2021. I clearly see a demonic looking face in the middle with what appears as horns around the face. There is another face to the bottom right as well.

Photo: This beautiful angel slyph face appeared above Prescott Valley, Arizona on July 5th, 2021.

Photo: This beautiful pair of kissing angel slyph faces appeared above St. Thomas Catholic Church in Tucson, Arizona on July 6th, 2021.

Photo: This beautiful sunset appeared above Tucson, Arizona on the evening of July 6th, 2021 while on my way to work with local retina surgeons.

Photo: This beautiful and huge angel slyph wing appeared above Prescott Valley, Arizona on July 6th, 2021 while entering St. Germaine Catholic Church for a morning mass.

Photo: This is a photo of massive wildfires in the Bradshaw Mountains north of Phoenix, Arizona. Wildfires have been a persistent problem in 2021 which saw record heat waves across the western states.

Photo: This beautiful angel slyph face with wings appeared above St. Thomas Catholic Church above Tucson, Arizona on July 7th, 2021 while on my way from working with local retina surgeons.

Photo: This beautiful angel slyph face appeared above St. Thomas Catholic Church above Tucson, Arizona on July 7th, 2021 while on my way from working with local retina surgeons.

Photo: This beautiful angel slyph face with wings appeared above St. Thomas Catholic Church above Tucson, Arizona on July 7th, 2021 while on my way from working with local retina surgeons.

Photo: This beautiful angel slyph face with wings appeared above Prescott Valley, Arizona following the passing of a good friend named Roger Dunigan on July 8th, 2021. I believe this is an actual photo of the angel responsible for taking Roger to heaven where he is watching over all of us.

Photo: This beautiful and mysterious angel slyph face with wings appeared at sunrise above Prescott Valley, Arizona on July 10th, 2021.

Photo: This beautiful and mysterious angel slyph face with wings appeared at sunrise above St. Germaine Catholic Church in Prescott Valley, Arizona on July 10th, 2021.

Photo: This beautiful and mysterious angel slyph face with wings appeared at sunrise above St. Germaine Catholic Church in Prescott Valley, Arizona on July 10th, 2021.

Photo: This beautiful and mysterious angel slyph pair of wings appeared to be surrounding a heart in Prescott Valley, Arizona on July 10th, 2021.

Photo: This beautiful and mysterious angel slyph face appeared to be hovering above Prescott Valley, Arizona on July 10th, 2021.

Photo: This beautiful and mysterious angel slyph wing appeared to be hovering above Prescott Valley, Arizona on July 10th, 2021.

Photo: This beautiful and mysterious angel slyph wing appeared above our home in Prescott Valley, Arizona on July 10th, 2021 after monsoon rains fell. You can see a face top right with right wing outstretched.

Photo: This beautiful and mysterious angel slyph wing appeared to be hovering above Prescott Valley, Arizona on July 10th, 2021. Soon after this appeared we had a heavy rainfall.

Photo: This beautiful and mysterious angel slyph wing appeared above our home in Prescott Valley, Arizona on July 10th, 2021 after monsoon rains fell. You can see a female face hovering top middle of the frame.

Photo: This beautiful and mysterious angel slyph head/face appeared to be hovering above Prescott Valley, Arizona on July 10th, 2021. Soon after this appeared we had a heavy rainfall.

Photo: This beautiful and mysterious angel slyph wing appeared above our home in Prescott Valley, Arizona on July 10th, 2021 after monsoon rains fell.

Photo: This beautiful and mysterious angel slyph appeared above our home in Prescott Valley, Arizona on July 10th, 2021 after monsoon rains fell. This one to me looks oddly like Nemo from Finding Nemo.

Photo: This beautiful and mysterious angel slyph wing with head and body appeared above our home in Prescott Valley, Arizona on July 10th, 2021 after monsoon rains fell. You can clearly see a head and face at top of a spine with wings outstretched.

Photo: This beautiful and mysterious angel slyph face appeared above our home in Prescott Valley, Arizona on July 11th, 2021. This oddly appeared to me like an Ewok from Star Wars.

Photo: This beautiful and mysterious angel slyph sunrise above our home in Prescott Valley, Arizona on July 12th, 2021.

Photo: This beautiful and mysterious angel slyph wing above our home in Prescott Valley, Arizona on July 12th, 2021.

Photo: A close up of the beautiful and mysterious angel slyph butterfly wing sunset above our home in Prescott Valley, Arizona on July 12th, 2021 as monsoon rains hit.

Photo: This beautiful and mysterious angel slyph sunrise above our home in Prescott Valley, Arizona on July 12th, 2021.

Photo: This beautiful and mysterious angel slyph head to the right looking to the left at a large wing above our home in Prescott Valley, Arizona on July 12th, 2021.

Photo: This beautiful and mysterious angel slyph sunrise appeared above our home in Prescott Valley, Arizona on the morning of July 13th, 2021.

Photo: This beautiful and mysterious angel slyph wing appeared above Durango, Colorado on July 14th, 2021 as I traveled to work with local retina surgeons.

Photo: This beautiful and mysterious angel slyph sunrise above Durango, Colorado on July 16th, 2021 as I left from there after working with local retina surgeons.

Photo: This beautiful and mysterious angel slyph sunrise above Durango, Colorado on July 16th, 2021 as I left from there after working with local retina surgeons.

Photo: This beautiful and mysterious angel slyph wing appeared near the Bradshaw Mountains near Phoenix, Arizona on July 16th, 2021.

Photo: This beautiful and mysterious angel slyph wing appeared above Phoenix, Arizona over the Bradshaw Mountains on July 16th, 2021. This was the site of a large wildfire earlier in the month. You can see amazingly a cross has formed in the middle of the wing.

Photo: This beautiful and mysterious row of angels hovered above Phoenix, Arizona on July 16th, 2021. I found this interesting because we had massive wildfires in the Bradshaw Mountains seen below a week earlier.

Photo: This beautiful and mysterious angel slyph wing appeared near the Bradshaw Mountains near Phoenix, Arizona on July 16th, 2021.

Photo: This beautiful and mysterious angel slyph figure appeared above our neighborhood in Prescott Valley, Arizona on July 16th, 2021.

Photo: This beautiful and mysterious angel slyph figure appeared above our neighborhood in Prescott Valley, Arizona on July 17th, 2021.

Photo: This beautiful and mysterious angel slyph figure appeared above our neighborhood in Prescott Valley, Arizona on July 17th, 2021.

Photo: This beautiful and mysterious angel slyph figure appeared above our neighborhood in Prescott Valley, Arizona on July 17th, 2021.

Photo: This beautiful and mysterious angel slyph figure appeared above our neighborhood in Prescott Valley, Arizona on July 17th, 2021. There is definitely a face staring up to the heavens.

Photo: This beautiful and mysterious angel slyph figure appeared above our neighborhood in Prescott Valley, Arizona on July 17th, 2021.

Photo: This beautiful and mysterious angel slyph figure appeared above our neighborhood in Prescott Valley, Arizona on July 17th, 2021. It appears to be looking up to the right toward heaven.

Photo: This beautiful and mysterious angel slyph figure appeared above our neighborhood in Prescott Valley, Arizona on July 17th, 2021.

Photo: This beautiful and mysterious angel slyph figure appeared above our neighborhood in Prescott Valley, Arizona on July 17th, 2021. You can clearly see a face looking down to the right.

Photo: This beautiful and mysterious angel slyph figure appeared above our neighborhood in Prescott Valley, Arizona on July 17th, 2021. You can clearly see a smiling face.

Photo: This beautiful and mysterious angel slyph figure appeared above our neighborhood in Prescott Valley, Arizona on July 17th, 2021. You can clearly see a face looking down the right of the frame.

Photo: This beautiful and mysterious angel slyph figure appeared above our neighborhood in Prescott Valley, Arizona on July 17th, 2021. You can clearly see a hovering figure with wings to the top left of the cloud.

Photo: This beautiful and mysterious angel slyph figure appeared above our neighborhood in Prescott Valley, Arizona on July 17th, 2021. You can clearly see a face looking down the left of the frame.

Photo: This beautiful and mysterious angel slyph figure appeared above our neighborhood in Prescott Valley, Arizona on July 17th, 2021. You can clearly see a face in the left of the frame.

Photo: This beautiful and mysterious angel slyph wing at sunset appeared above our neighborhood in Prescott Valley, Arizona on July 17th, 2021 as my wife and I celebrated our 13th year wedding anniversary.

Photo: This beautiful and mysterious angel slyph figure appeared above our neighborhood in Prescott Valley, Arizona on July 18th, 2021. You can clearly see two faces and heads top right of the frame.

Photo: This beautiful and mysterious angel slyph wing and face appeared above our neighborhood in Prescott Valley, Arizona on July 18th, 2021. You can clearly see a face down to the left of the frame.

Photo: This beautiful and mysterious angel slyph figure appeared above our neighborhood in Prescott Valley, Arizona on July 18th, 2021.

Photo: This beautiful and mysterious angel slyph figure and wing appeared above our neighborhood in Prescott Valley, Arizona on July 18th, 2021. You can clearly see a face looking to the left of the frame.

THE BLUE LADY

The image is an image of what I call, 'The Blue Lady'. After seeing such an incredible sight, I decided to name this book after my experience.

Let me explain why I chose this image for the cover. As I mentioned in previous books, I believe myself to be reincarnation of James Douglas Morrison, former lead singer of the classic rock band The Doors.

Before Jim's untimely death in 1971, he wrote a screenplay called 'The Blue Lady'. Many of his closest friends believed it was about his blue corvette, which he nicknamed The Blue Lady.

As most of Jim's lyrics and poems had multiple meanings. In this case, I believe he foresaw (as he was a Prophet of Mary) this apparition of The Blue Lady in his next life with me.

In my previous books, I explained that Jim and I are the left and right jaw respectively of St. Mary. He used to refer to us as spiritually conjoined and as "lurking jaws, joints in time."

So, if any fans of Jim are reading this by chance, no he is not dead, and here is Jim's Blue Lady.

Photo: This blue lady with red wings and a long blue face appeared in our skies on July 18th, 2021 as I walked our dog Reese with my wife Carol Rose.

Photo: A great photo of James Douglas Morrison sometime near 1970 as he was the lead singer of The Doors musical group. This is my fraternal twin and the left jaw of St. Mary, a Prophet of God. My previous books have decoded many of his lyrics and prophecies and showed how they were all recently fulfilled on earth.

Photo: The right jaw of St. Mary and also prophet Matthew Douglas Pinard in 2020 and author of these books and the new wine book series. I have the same mole on my left cheek and same middle name as the left jaw James Douglas Morrison. I can also hit every note he recorded and also knew all of the lyrics the first time I heard them.

Photo: This beautiful and mysterious angel slyph figure appeared above our neighborhood in Prescott Valley, Arizona on July 18th, 2021. You can clearly see a face top middle.

Photo: This beautiful and mysterious angel slyph figure appeared above our neighborhood in Prescott Valley, Arizona on July 18th, 2021. You can clearly see a face in the middle.

Photo: This beautiful and mysterious angel slyph wing appeared above Prescott Valley, Arizona on July 18th, 2021. I see a cross in the middle of the frame.

Photo: This beautiful and mysterious angel slyph figure appeared above our neighborhood in Prescott Valley, Arizona on July 18th, 2021.

Photo: This beautiful and mysterious angel slyph figure appeared above our neighborhood in Prescott Valley, Arizona on July 18th, 2021.

Photo: This beautiful and mysterious angel slyph figure appeared above our neighborhood in Prescott Valley, Arizona on July 18th, 2021.

Photo: This beautiful and mysterious angel slyph figure appeared above our neighborhood in Prescott Valley, Arizona on July 18th, 2021. I see what appears to be a dog's face to the top left of the frame.

Photo: This beautiful and mysterious angel slyph wing appeared above St. Germaine Catholic Church in Prescott Valley, Arizona on July 18th, 2021.

Photo: This beautiful and mysterious angel slyph wing appeared above Prescott Valley, Arizona on July 18th, 2021.

Photo: This beautiful and mysterious angel slyph wing appeared above our home in Prescott Valley, Arizona on July 18th, 2021.

Photo: This beautiful and mysterious angel slyph wing appeared above our home in Prescott Valley, Arizona on July 18th, 2021.

Photo: This beautiful and mysterious angel slyph wing appeared above our home in Prescott Valley, Arizona on July 18th, 2021. You can see a huge horned head to the top right.

Photo: This beautiful and mysterious angel slyph wing appeared above Prescott Valley, Arizona on July 18th, 2021.

Photo: This beautiful and mysterious angel slyph head appeared above our home in Prescott Valley, Arizona on July 18th, 2021. You can see a huge horned head.

Photo: This beautiful and mysterious angel slyph wing appeared above our home in Prescott Valley, Arizona on July 19th, 2021.

Photo: This beautiful and mysterious angel slyph wing appeared above our home in Prescott Valley, Arizona on July 18th, 2021.

Photo: This beautiful and mysterious angel slyph wing and face appeared above our home in Prescott Valley, Arizona on July 18th, 2021.

Photo: This beautiful and mysterious angel slyph wing appeared above our home in Prescott Valley, Arizona on July 19th, 2021.

Photo: This beautiful and mysterious angel slyph wing appeared above our home in Prescott Valley, Arizona on July 19th, 2021.

Photo: This beautiful and mysterious angel slyph wing appeared above our home in Prescott Valley, Arizona on July 19th, 2021.

Photo: This beautiful and mysterious angel slyph wing appeared above our home in Prescott Valley, Arizona on July 19th, 2021. There is a definite face in the middle.

Photo: This beautiful and mysterious angel slyph wing appeared above our home in Prescott Valley, Arizona on July 19th, 2021.

Photo: This beautiful and mysterious angel slyph wing and face appeared above our home in Prescott Valley, Arizona on July 19th, 2021.

Photo: This beautiful and mysterious angel slyph bowing appeared above our home in Prescott Valley, Arizona on July 19th, 2021.

Photo: This beautiful and mysterious angel slyph wing appeared above our home in Prescott Valley, Arizona on July 19th, 2021.

Photo: This beautiful and mysterious angel slyph winged sunset appeared above our home in Prescott Valley, Arizona on July 19th, 2021.

Photo: This beautiful and mysterious angel slyph wing appeared above a local church in Prescott Valley, Arizona on July 19th, 2021.

Photo: This beautiful and mysterious angel slyph sunrise appeared near our home in Prescott Valley, Arizona on July 20th, 2021.

Photo: This beautiful and mysterious angel slyph blue turtle figure appeared above our home in Prescott Valley, Arizona on July 20th, 2021.

Photo: This beautiful and mysterious angel slyph wing appeared above our home in Prescott Valley, Arizona on July 20th, 2021.

Photo: This beautiful and mysterious angel slyph wing appeared above our home in Prescott Valley, Arizona on July 20th, 2021.

Photo: This beautiful and mysterious angel slyph wing appeared above our home in Prescott Valley, Arizona on July 20th, 2021.

Photo: This beautiful and mysterious angel slyph wing and head appeared above our home in Prescott Valley, Arizona on July 20th, 2021.

Photo: This beautiful and mysterious angel slyph wing appeared above our home in Prescott Valley, Arizona on July 20th, 2021.

Photo: This beautiful and mysterious angel slyph wing and face appeared above our home in Prescott Valley, Arizona on July 20th, 2021.

Photo: This beautiful and mysterious angel slyph wing appeared above our home in Prescott Valley, Arizona on July 20th, 2021.

Photo: This beautiful and mysterious angel slyph appeared above our home in Prescott Valley, Arizona on July 20th, 2021. It appears to be kneeling in prayer hands folded.

Photo: This beautiful and mysterious angel slyph wing appeared above our home in Prescott Valley, Arizona on July 20th, 2021.

Photo: This beautiful and mysterious angel slyph wing and face appeared above our home in Prescott Valley, Arizona on July 20th, 2021. Shortly after this appearance large monsoon rains hit central Arizona.

Photo: This beautiful and mysterious angel slyph wing sunset appeared above Kingman, Arizona on July 20th, 2021. This is one of the most beautiful photos I've ever taken.

Photo: This beautiful and mysterious angel slyph wing sunrise appeared above Kingman, Arizona on July 21st, 2021.

Photo: This beautiful and mysterious angel slyph wing and face appeared above Las Vegas, Nevada on July 21st, 2021. This appeared above a surgery center where I was working with local retina surgeons.

Photo: This beautiful and mysterious angel slyph wing appeared above Las Vegas, Nevada on July 21st, 2021. This appeared above a surgery center where I was working with local retina surgeons.

Photo: This beautiful and mysterious angel slyph wing and face appeared above Las Vegas, Nevada on July 21st, 2021. This appeared above a surgery center where I was working with local retina surgeons.

Photo: This beautiful and mysterious angel slyph wing and face appeared above Las Vegas, Nevada on July 21st, 2021. This appeared above a surgery center where I was working with local retina surgeons.

Photo: This beautiful and mysterious angel slyph wing and face appeared above Las Vegas, Nevada on July 21st, 2021. This appeared above a surgery center where I was working with local retina surgeons.

Photo: This beautiful and mysterious angel slyph wing and face appeared above Las Vegas, Nevada on July 22nd, 2021. This appeared above a surgery center where I was working with local retina surgeons.

Photo: This beautiful and mysterious angel slyph wing and face appeared above Las Vegas, Nevada on July 21st, 2021. This appeared above a surgery center where I was working with local retina surgeons.

Photo: This beautiful and mysterious angel slyph wing and face appeared above Las Vegas, Nevada on July 21st, 2021. This appeared above a surgery center where I was working with local retina surgeons.

Photo: This beautiful and mysterious angel slyph appeared above Las Vegas, Nevada on July 22nd, 2021. This appeared above a surgery center where I was working with local retina surgeons.

Photo: This beautiful and mysterious angel slyph wing appeared above Las Vegas, Nevada on July 22nd, 2021. This appeared above a surgery center where I was working with local retina surgeons.

Photo: This beautiful and mysterious angel slyph wing and face appeared above Las Vegas, Nevada on July 22nd, 2021. This appeared above a surgery center where I was working with local retina surgeons.

Photo: This beautiful and mysterious angel slyph wing and face appeared above Las Vegas, Nevada on July 22nd, 2021. I can clearly see a face looking down to the right.

Photo: This beautiful and mysterious angel slyph wing appeared above our home in Prescott Valley, Arizona on July 24th, 2021.

Photo: This beautiful and mysterious angel slyph wing appeared above our home in Prescott Valley, Arizona on July 24th, 2021.

Photo: This beautiful and mysterious angel slyph wing appeared above our home in Prescott Valley, Arizona on July 24th, 2021. I can see two faces below an elephant head top middle of the frame.

Photo: This beautiful and mysterious angel slyph wing appeared above our home in Prescott Valley, Arizona on July 24th, 2021.

Photo: This beautiful and mysterious angel slyph wing and face appeared above our home in Prescott Valley, Arizona on July 24th, 2021.

Photo: This beautiful and mysterious angel slyph wing appeared above our home in Prescott Valley, Arizona on July 24th, 2021. This looks like an angel holding a baby angel.

Photo: This beautiful and mysterious angel slyph flying from the right to the left appeared above our home in Prescott Valley, Arizona on July 24th, 2021.

Photo: This beautiful and mysterious angel slyph wing appeared above our home in Prescott Valley, Arizona on July 24th, 2021.

Photo: This beautiful and mysterious angel slyph wing appeared above our home in Prescott Valley, Arizona on July 24th, 2021.

Photo: This beautiful and mysterious blue angel slyph wing appeared above our home in Prescott Valley, Arizona on July 24th, 2021.

Photo: This beautiful and mysterious angel slyph wing appeared above our home in Prescott Valley, Arizona on July 24th, 2021.

Photo: This beautiful and mysterious angel slyph wing appeared above our home in Prescott Valley, Arizona on July 24th, 2021.

Photo: This beautiful and mysterious angel slyph wing and face appeared above our home in Prescott Valley, Arizona on July 24th, 2021.

Photo: This beautiful and mysterious angel slyph wing with four heads appeared above Sacred Heart Catholic Church in Prescott, Arizona on July 25th, 2021.

Photo: This beautiful and mysterious angel slyph wing and face appeared above Sacred Heart Catholic Church in Prescott, Arizona on July 25th, 2021.

Photo: This beautiful and mysterious angel slyph wing and face appeared above Sacred Heart Catholic Church in Prescott, Arizona on July 25th, 2021.

Photo: On July 25th, 2021 this powerful meteor exploded over Norway further confirmation we are in an apocalypse in hopes of preventing another world war. An apocalypse could mean a new beginning for the world. Let's hope and pray that it does.

Photo: This incredible angel slyph figure appeared above our neighborhood in Prescott Valley, Arizona on July 26th, 2021. You can clearly see what looks like a chipmunk head top left and a wing behind to the top right of the frame.

Photo: On July 26th, 2021 this beautiful angel slyph appeared in our neighborhood in Prescott Valley, Arizona. I see what appears to be a small dog to the left of the frame.

Photo: On July 26th, 2021 this beautiful angel slyph appeared in our neighborhood in Prescott Valley, Arizona. I see what appears to be a head to the left of the frame.

Photo: On July 26th, 2021 these two angel slyph faces appeared behind our house in Prescott Valley, Arizona.

Photo: On July 26th, 2021 our friend Sherri captured this amazing photo of a smiling face angel slyph above Prescott, Arizona.

Photo: On July 26th, 2021 this beautiful angel slyph appeared in our neighborhood in Prescott Valley, Arizona. I see what appears to be a large face top middle of the frame.

Photo: On July 26th, 2021 this beautiful angel slyph appeared in our neighborhood in Prescott Valley, Arizona. I see what appears to be a face looking to the left of the frame.

Photo: On July 26th, 2021 this beautiful angel slyph appeared in our neighborhood in Prescott Valley, Arizona. I see what appears to be two heads and also what looks like a subtly forming cross.

Photo: On July 26th, 2021 this beautiful angel slyph appeared in our neighborhood in Prescott Valley, Arizona. I see what appears to be a head in the middle of the frame with a wing protruding out.

Photo: On July 26th, 2021 this beautiful angel slyph appeared in our neighborhood in Prescott Valley, Arizona. I see what appears to be a two faces staring at each other above a blue two headed angel with legs.

Photo: On July 26th, 2021 this beautiful angel slyph appeared in our neighborhood in Prescott Valley, Arizona. I see what appears to be a multiple angel slyph faces, can you pick them out?

Photo: On July 26th, 2021 this beautiful angel slyph appeared in our neighborhood in Prescott Valley, Arizona. I see what appears to be a a smiling face mouth open to the right staring at floating slyphs to the left.

Photo: On July 26th, 2021 this beautiful angel slyph appeared in our neighborhood in Prescott Valley, Arizona. I see what appears to be a two faces looking in opposite directions.

Photo: On July 26th, 2021 this beautiful angel slyph appeared in our neighborhood in Prescott Valley, Arizona. I see what appears to be multiple faces, can you pick them out?

Photo: On July 27th, 2021 this beautiful angel slyph wing appeared in our neighborhood in Prescott Valley, Arizona.

Photo: On July 26th, 2021 this beautiful angel slyph appeared in our neighborhood in Prescott Valley, Arizona. I see what appears to be a large blue angel slyph face in the middle of the frame.

Photo: On July 26th, 2021 this beautiful angel slyph appeared in our neighborhood in Prescott Valley, Arizona. I see what appears to be a large head to the middle of the frame.

Photo: On July 28th, 2021 this beautiful angel slyph wing with faces appeared in our neighborhood in Prescott Valley, Arizona.

Photo: On July 28th, 2021 this beautiful angel slyph wing appeared above Salt Lake City, Utah while working with local retina surgeons.

Photo: On July 28th, 2021 this beautiful angel slyph wing with huge face appeared above Salt Lake City, Utah while working with local retina surgeons.

Photo: On July 28th, 2021 this beautiful angel slyph wing with faces appeared in our neighborhood in Prescott Valley, Arizona.

Photo: On July 28th, 2021 this beautiful angel slyph wing appeared above Salt Lake City, Utah while working with local retina surgeons.

Photo: On July 28th, 2021 this beautiful angel slyph wing with face appeared above Salt Lake City, Utah while working with local retina surgeons.

Photo: On July 28th, 2021 this beautiful angel slyph wing and face appeared above Salt Lake City, Utah while working with local retina surgeons.

Photo: On July 29th, 2021 this beautiful angel slyph wing and face appeared above Salt Lake City, Utah while working with local retina surgeons. This was directly above a children's hospital.

Photo: On July 29th, 2021 this beautiful angel slyph wing and face appeared above Salt Lake City, Utah while working with local retina surgeons. This was directly above a children's hospital.

Photo: On July 29th, 2021 this beautiful angel slyph wing and face appeared above Salt Lake City, Utah while working with local retina surgeons.

Photo: On July 29th, 2021 this beautiful angel slyph wing appeared above Salt Lake City, Utah while working with local retina surgeons.

Photo: On July 29th, 2021 this beautiful angel slyph wing appeared above Salt Lake City, Utah while working with local retina surgeons. Notice the bright blue orb to the left of the sun.

Photo: On July 29th, 2021 this beautiful angel slyph wing appeared above Salt Lake City, Utah while working with local retina surgeons.

Photo: On July 29th, 2021 this beautiful angel slyph wing and large face appeared above Salt Lake City, Utah while working with local retina surgeons.

Photo: On July 30th, 2021 this beautiful angel slyph double wing appeared above Phoenix, Arizona.

Photo: On July 30th, 2021 this beautiful angel slyph double wing appeared above Phoenix, Arizona.

Photo: On July 30th, 2021 this beautiful angel slyph double wing appeared above Phoenix, Arizona.

Photo: On July 30th, 2021 this beautiful angel slyph wing and face appeared above Phoenix, Arizona.

Photo: On July 30th, 2021 this beautiful angel slyph appeared above Phoenix, Arizona. If you look closely you can see a female face top left.

Photo: On July 30th, 2021 this beautiful angel slyph wing and face appeared above Phoenix, Arizona.

Photo: On July 30th, 2021 this beautiful angel slyph wing appeared above Phoenix, Arizona.

Photo: On July 30th, 2021 this beautiful angel slyph wing appeared above Phoenix, Arizona.

Photo: On July 30th, 2021 this beautiful angel slyph wing appeared above Phoenix, Arizona.

Photo: On July 30th, 2021 this beautiful angel slyph appeared above Phoenix, Arizona.

Photo: On July 30th, 2021 this beautiful angel slyph appeared above Phoenix, Arizona. Can you see multiple faces/heads too?

Photo: On July 30th, 2021 this beautiful angel slyph wing appeared above Phoenix, Arizona.

Photo: On July 30th, 2021 this beautiful angel slyph appeared above Prescott Valley, Arizona at sunset.

Photo: On July 30th, 2021 this beautiful angel slyph wing appeared at sunset above Prescott Valley, Arizona.

Photo: On July 30th, 2021 this beautiful angel slyph sunset appeared above Prescott Valley, Arizona.

Photo: On July 30th, 2021 this beautiful angel slyph face sunset appeared above Prescott Valley, Arizona.

Photo: On July 30th, 2021 this beautiful angel slyph face appeared above Prescott Valley, Arizona at dusk.

Photo: On July 30th, 2021 this beautiful angel slyph face appeared above Prescott Valley, Arizona. Can you see a face with a beard to the right?

Photo: On July 30th, 2021 this beautiful angel slyph appeared above Prescott Valley, Arizona. Can you see a face far left?

Photo: On July 30th, 2021 this beautiful angel slyph flying to the left appeared above Prescott Valley, Arizona.

Photo: On July 31st, 2021 this beautiful angel slyph wing and face appeared above a dojo I teach ancient Samurai JuJutsu at in Prescott, Arizona.

Photo: On July 31st, 2021 this beautiful angel slyph wing and face appeared above Prescott, Arizona.

Photo: On July 31st, 2021 this beautiful angel slyph wing and face appeared above Prescott, Arizona.

Photo: On July 31st, 2021 this beautiful angel slyph wing and face appeared above Prescott, Arizona.

Photo: On July 31st, 2021 this beautiful angel slyph wing and face appeared above Prescott, Arizona.

Photo: On July 31st, 2021 this beautiful angel slyph wing and face appeared above Prescott, Arizona. There is a huge face to the bottom left of the sun.

Photo: On July 31st, 2021 this beautiful angel slyph wing and face appeared above Prescott, Arizona. You can clearly see a large face to the far left.

Photo: On July 31st, 2021 this beautiful angel slyph wing and face appeared above Prescott, Arizona. You can clearly see a large face to the far left.

Photo: On July 31st, 2021 this beautiful angel slyph wing and face appeared above Prescott, Arizona. You can clearly see a large face to the right of the frame.

Photo: On July 31st, 2021 this beautiful angel slyph wing and face appeared above Prescott, Arizona. You can clearly see a large face to the right of the frame.

Photo: On July 31st, 2021 this beautiful angel slyph wing and face appeared above Prescott, Arizona.

Photo: On July 31st, 2021 this beautiful angel slyph wing appeared above Prescott, Arizona. You can clearly see a large "Z" in the middle of the frame. This "Z" angel is dedicated to my friend Jaqueline Zralka, an amazing spiritual teacher, angel channeler and clairvoyant who will soon be an author of books with photos even better than mine (I've seen some of them).

Photo: On July 31st, 2021 this beautiful angel slyph wing and face appeared above Prescott, Arizona. You can clearly see a large face to the middle of the frame.

Photo: On July 31st, 2021 this beautiful angel slyph wing and face appeared above Prescott Valley, Arizona at sunset.

Photo: On July 31st, 2021 this beautiful angel slyph wing and face appeared above Prescott, Arizona.

Photo: On July 31st, 2021 this beautiful angel slyph wing and face appeared above Prescott, Arizona. This appears to be forming a cross as well.

Photo: On July 31st, 2021 this beautiful angel slyph wing and face appeared above Prescott, Arizona.

Photo: On July 31st, 2021 this beautiful angel slyph wing and face appeared above Prescott, Arizona. You can clearly see a large face on a figure walking to the left.

Photo: On July 31st, 2021 this beautiful angel slyph sunset appeared above Prescott Valley, Arizona.

Photo: On July 31st, 2021 this beautiful angel slyph wing and face appeared above Prescott Valley, Arizona at sunset.

Photo: On July 31st, 2021 this beautiful angel slyph wing appeared above Prescott Valley, Arizona at sunset.

Photo: On July 31st, 2021 this beautiful angel slyph sunset appeared above Prescott Valley, Arizona.

Photo: On July 31st, 2021 this beautiful angel slyph wing and face appeared above Prescott Valley, Arizona at sunset. This appears to me as a mother angel holding a baby angel.

Photo: On July 31st, 2021 this beautiful angel slyph appeared above Prescott Valley, Arizona at sunset. This appears to me as a mother angel holding a baby angel.

THE AUGUST SLYPHS AND A FEW DEMONS

I want to take a moment to document something that occurred to my wife Carol Rose and I while having Sunday morning breakfast at our favorite local diner in Prescott, Arizona.

We just attended a local mass service at Sacred Heart Catholic Church on Sunday, August 1st, 2021. I probably would have walked past the items I am about to show you, but having just been at church, it was probably more "spiritually awake" than normal.

In any event, I noticed three strategically placed items in the restaurant/coffee shop that were very revealing, to say the least. I will explain in more detail below.

Photo: A statue of a fallen angel or demon found near where people place their food and coffee orders in Prescott, Arizona. I noticed this piece of artwork while having breakfast with my wife Carol Rose after church. Such an object could bring actual demons into our world.

Photo: A third piece of artwork for sale entitled "Captain Kiowa" as seen in a local eatery in Prescott, Arizona on August 1st, 2021. Such a piece of artwork could serve to bring actual fallen angels/demons into our world. This piece is especially interesting to me because historically Kiowa was an Apache Indian at the massacre of Salt Creek.

Photo: A second piece of artwork for sale entitled "stolen from Dracula" as seen in a local eatery in Prescott, Arizona on August 1st, 2021. Such a piece of artwork could serve to bring actual fallen angels/ demons into our world.

The three statues seemed strategically placed as innocuous decorations, "harmless." However, the evidence tells another tale. In my experience over the last several years, there is a worldwide spiritual battle between God, the Devil, Angels and Demons. Therefore, I pray daily that the kingdom of light prevails, as these fallen entities want nothing but suffering for you and your loved ones.

Photo: A "burning bush" from wildfires on Hawaii in early August, 2021. This image immediately brought to mind the biblical story of the burning bush where God talked to mankind. Do you think he's trying to reach us now?

Photo: This incredible angel slyph wing and faces appeared above Prescott Valley, Arizona on August 1st, 2021.

Photo: This incredible angel slyph wing appeared above Prescott Valley, Arizona on August 1st, 2021.

Photo: This incredible angel slyph wing appeared above Prescott Valley, Arizona on August 1st, 2021.

Photo: This incredible angel slyph double wing appeared above Prescott Valley, Arizona on August 1st, 2021.

Photo: This incredible angel slyph wing appeared above Prescott Valley, Arizona on August 1st, 2021. You can see a face to the left of the blue angel.

Photo: This incredible angel slyph wing appeared above Prescott Valley, Arizona on August 1st, 2021.

Photo: This incredible angel slyph wing appeared above Sacred Heart Catholic Church in Prescott Valley, Arizona on August 1st, 2021.

Photo: This incredible angel slyph wing and face appeared above Prescott Valley, Arizona on August 1st, 2021.

Photo: This incredible angel slyph wing and face appeared above Prescott Valley, Arizona on August 1st, 2021.

Photo: This incredible angel slyph wing and face appeared above Prescott Valley, Arizona on August 1st, 2021.

Photo: This incredible angel slyph wing and face appeared above Prescott Valley, Arizona on August 1st, 2021.

Photo: This incredible angel slyph wing and face appeared above Prescott Valley, Arizona on August 1st, 2021.

Photo: This incredible angel slyph wing appeared above Prescott Valley, Arizona on August 1st, 2021.

Photo: This incredible angel slyph wing appeared above Prescott Valley, Arizona on August 1st, 2021.

Photo: This incredible angel slyph wing appeared above Prescott Valley, Arizona on August 1st, 2021.

Photo: This incredible angel slyph wing and face appeared above Prescott Valley, Arizona on August 1st, 2021.

Photo: This incredible angel slyph wing and face appeared above Prescott Valley, Arizona on August 1st, 2021. I see in the middle what appears to be a cross lit by the sun.

Photo: This incredible angel slyph wing and face appeared above Prescott Valley, Arizona on August 1st, 2021.

Photo: This incredible angel slyph wing and face appeared above Prescott Valley, Arizona on August 1st, 2021. This looks like one angel above another.

Photo: This incredible angel slyph wing and face appeared above Prescott Valley, Arizona on August 1st, 2021. This looks like an angel flying backwards.

Photo: This incredible angel slyph wing and face appeared above Prescott Valley, Arizona on August 1st, 2021.

Photo: This incredible angel slyph wing and face appeared above Prescott Valley, Arizona on August 1st, 2021.

Photo: This incredible angel slyph wing and face appeared above Prescott Valley, Arizona on August 1st, 2021.

Photo: This incredible angel slyph wing and face appeared above Prescott Valley, Arizona on August 1st, 2021.

Photo: This incredible angel slyph wing and face appeared above Prescott Valley, Arizona on August 1st, 2021.

Photo: This incredible angel slyph appeared above Prescott Valley, Arizona on August 1st, 2021. This appears as if the angel is reaching out to the bottom left of the frame.

Photo: This incredible angel slyph wing and face appeared above Prescott Valley, Arizona on August 1st, 2021. You can see a face to the far left and two wings to the right.

Photo: This incredible angel slyph wing and face appeared above Prescott Valley, Arizona on August 1st, 2021. I see two faces staring at each other.

Photo: This incredible angel slyph choir appeared above Prescott Valley, Arizona on August 1st, 2021.

Photo: This incredible angel slyph wing and two faces with twin rainbows appeared above Prescott Valley, Arizona on August 1st, 2021.

Photo: This incredible angel slyph wing and face appeared above Prescott Valley, Arizona on August 1st, 2021. You can see an angel slyph at the top of the cloud and a glimpse of heaven below.

Photo: This incredible angel slyph face next to a rainbow appeared above Prescott Valley, Arizona on August 1st, 2021.

Photo: This incredible angel slyph wing and face next to a faint rainbow appeared above Prescott Valley, Arizona on August 1st, 2021.

Photo: This incredible angel sunset appeared above Prescott Valley, Arizona on August 1st, 2021.

Photo: This incredible angel slyph winged sunset appeared above Prescott Valley, Arizona on August 1st, 2021.

Photo: This incredible angel slyph winged sunset appeared above a local church near Prescott Valley, Arizona on August 1st, 2021.

Photo: This incredible angel slyph sunset appeared above Prescott Valley, Arizona on August 1st, 2021.

Photo: This incredible angel slyph sunset appeared above Prescott Valley, Arizona on August 1st, 2021.

Photo: This incredible angel slyph sunset appeared above Prescott Valley, Arizona on August 1st, 2021.

Photo: This incredible angel slyph sunset appeared above Prescott Valley, Arizona on August 1st, 2021. This clearly appears to me as if a female angel slyph is blowing a row of sunlit kisses to the male angel slyph to the right.

MEET VIRGINIA

I want to take a moment towards the end of this book to introduce a wonderful woman named Virginia Simonin from Portland, Oregon. Virginia is a member (as am I) of an Angel Facebook group.

Virginia posted asking for psychic assistance to help locate her son Sean Simonin, who lived on the streets.

After a rosary at a local Catholic Church, explained my vision of seeing an image of a tan corded telephone hanging on a wall and a child's stuffed dinosaur.

Once she confirmed the phone, saying they had one like that when Sean was a young boy. Virginia also told me Sean had a stuffed dinosaur when he was young.

I knew by my prayer session; Sean was abused by an older child when he was young. She also confirmed.

Then, I also saw an image of jazz players on Beale Street in Memphis. Virginia said her son never mentioned anything about my vision, but loved music.

Virginia called me a few weeks later to say she had located Sean in downtown Portland, Oregon. She was thankful they were reunited and happy.

My vision, which showed him as still living, was, in fact, accurate. Virginia stated she said a full rosary, asking the many Angel Sylph's in the skies to help find her son. During our conversation, I had explained how to say a rosary. To date, Virginia was able to reunite Sean with his father, and she still holds hope for him to come home.

Photo: A recent photo of a new angel friend Virginia Simonin who enlisted my psychic/clairvoyance assistance to locate her son Sean mid-2021.

Photo: An earlier photo of Sean Simonin, a young man living on the streets who's mother asked for help in locating him mid 2021.

CONCLUSION

In conclusion, I want to express my belief in what is happening to our world.

The universe is a multi-dimensional multi-verse with many worlds, species and races of God's creation. I recently read that some scientific experts predict a total societal collapse by 2040 if we do not immediately change things on this planet.

We can have fully electric vehicles, eliminating the need for fossil fuels, other than it is profitable for oil companies. Nor is there reason for WWIII… However, it would most likely collapse the world much sooner than 2040.

In the last few years, we have seen incredibly miraculous events, which I have tried to document in my books for all to see, read, and hear about. There is no doubt a God, a Heaven, angels, Mother Mary, and sadly a Devil.

It is humans' responsibility to collectively protect the Earth. No one person is greater than the next; we are all responsible for creating a brighter future for the young lives that now populate this planet in the billions.

My prayer is that the world wakes up and sees something more powerful than us, but a being that will not abandon us, especially now when this planet teeters on the brink of destruction.

If you would like to learn how to access these angels, Sylph's and The Blue Lady bring your spirit to a higher plane of living. Please contact me….

God Bless us all, and may he not abandon us in the middle of this dark night we are all living through.

I would like to finish this book with an original poem titled "The Blue Lady."

The Blue *Lady* (an original poem)

A ring of fire eclipses the night as twenty-seven vents unleash apocalyptic fire around the Pacific Rim

Slippery Sylphs slide through our skies signaling more horses seemingly on their mark

Monsoon rains quench scorched earth as one named done again rides on high towards the brim

The world's True King lies restlessly beneath pyramids pointing towards Orion's Lark

High crosses appear amongst pillowed clouds an exorcism of the fallen now enshrouds

Millions of acres burning through the night from record heats falling on deaf ears and minds

Those with billions seek to escape and slip the earthly bounds of this new found hell into clouds

As sunlit sprites fly down from places we do not see, but know there is a crown like colored citrus rinds

Heart shaped clouds precede arches wings as trumpets blare yet no one seems to hear their sound

Blue angel wings and faces hover unfettered across the skies screaming for their mention

Blanketing a hundred miles showing paranormal is the new normal hounding like a hound

A butterfly appears at sunset flapping wings of change as heavy rains pour over my attention

MoJo's Blue Lady appears her magenta wings spread across the frame a blue flame her crown

An army of her flying flock not fallen, not bound, yearning to free us all from the one with no illumination

"Wake up" she screams at her lions of the light, fight now to put an end to disbelief, as it's Satan's frown

Streaking meteor over the night of Norway signals a fire and fury that's but a preview for all called a nation

About the Author

Catholic Mystic and award-winning author and screenwriter Matthew Douglas Pinard is the author of seven books on angels, the afterlife, psychic clairvoyance, prophecy, and miraculous healing.

- Have you ever felt a presence you knew wanted something from you?
- Have you ever felt like you had a gift "locked", which was meant to bring light to this world?
- Have you ever witnessed an actual miracle of healing?
- Have you ever seen what you were convinced was a letter, animal, object, or angel in the skies?
- Are you concerned with the current course the world is on?

Matthew will help you communicate with loved ones who have passed and are angel spirit guides to protect and help us navigate this world.

The author explains his encounter with "The Woman Clothed with the Sun." He became a witness to an amazing precious blood miracle the Vatican is now investigating. It preceded three amazing healing miracles of degenerative diseases among friends and family.

Matthew's photographs will send chills down your spine, proving life exists in other dimensions outside the physical realm. This is a once-in-a-lifetime chance to unlock the deepest mysteries of your own life, bringing this world closer to peace, light, healing, and hope.

Matthew Douglas Pinard (formerly James Douglas Morrison)

734.649.8431 / pinardm@gmail.com / www.jimsnewwine.com

Other Books by Author Matthew Douglas Piard

matthewpinardauthor.com

Follow Me:

- Goodreads
- Author Central
- YouTube

@matthewpinardauthor.com

MATTHEW DOUGLAS PINARD

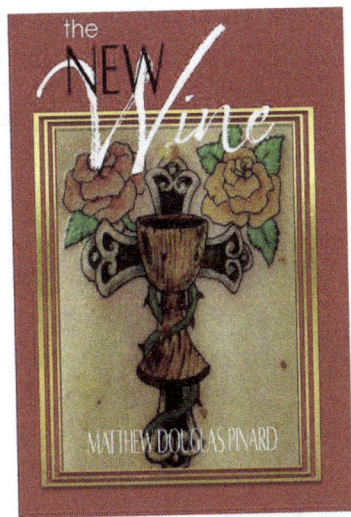

Screenplay Awards Matthew Douglas Pinard

Official Selection

    Bloodstained Indie Film Festival

    StoryPros Awards Screenplay Contest

    Military Script Showcase

    L.A. Neo Noir Novel Film & Script Festival

    True Story International Film Festival

    Reel Heart International Film Festival

    Hollywood Boulevard International Film Festival

    Independent Talents International Film Festival

    Fort Worth Indie Film Showcase

    California Independent Film Festival

    San Pedro International Film Festival,

    Southeastern International Film Festival

    Louisiana International Film Festival

Official Selection

First Ten Pages Script Contest

Atlanta Comedy Film Festival

Georgia Shorts Film Festival

Official Finalist

Las Vegas International Film and Screenwriting Contest, Honorable Mention

Depth of Field International Film Festival, Award Winner

Beverly Hills International Film Festival, Silver Winner

Queen Palm International Film Festival, Award Winner

Colorado International Film Festival, Quarter-Finalist

Chicago Screenplay Awards, Quarter-Finalist

NYC International Screenplay Awards, Quarter-Finalist

Atlanta Screenplay Awards, Semi-Finalist

Cordillera International Film Festival, Semi-Finalist

Fade In Awards, Finalist

Breaking Walls Thriller Screenplay Award Winner

Vegas Movie Awards,

The Santa Barbara International Screenplay Awards, Finalist

Miami Screen Play Awards, Quarter-Finalist:

www.ingramcontent.com/pod-product-compliance
Lightning Source LLC
Chambersburg PA
CBHW081352070526
44583CB00020B/2526